Stop Stressing About Dressing

Scarlett De Bease

Illustrations by Erica Liu

Copyright © 2016 by Scarlett De Bease
All rights reserved.

Green Ivy Publishing
1 Lincoln Centre
18W140 Butterfield Road
Suite 1500
Oakbrook Terrace IL 60181-4843
www.greenivybooks.com

ISBN: 978-1-945058-93-6

Contents

Chapter One - Stop Stressing About Dressing	1
Chapter Two - Push 'Em Up!	3
Chapter Three - If Not Now, When?	4
Chapter Four - Come Clean With Color	6
Chapter Five - Fabric Or Facelift?	8
Chapter Six - Let Your Hair Choose What To Wear	10
Chapter Seven - Are You A V-Neck Or Round-Neck?	12
Chapter Eight - Have Your Contents Shifted?	13
Chapter Nine - Size Doesn't Matter	15
Chapter Ten - End The Trend	17
Chapter Eleven - Don't Shop 'Til You Drop	19
Chapter Twelve - Do You Know Where Your Breasts Are?	22
Chapter Thirteen - The Perils Of High Heels	25
Chapter Fourteen - Step Back From The Rack	27
Chapter Fifteen - Divorce, Despair And What To Wear	29
Chapter Sixteen - Battling The Bathing Suit Blues	32
Chapter Seventeen - Don't Waste Your Waist	34
Chapter Eighteen - Where Have All The Sleeves Gone?	36
Before After	38, 39
Chapter Nineteen - Back Bumps And Lumps	40
Chapter 20 - Frumpy Or Fabulous?	42
Chapter Twenty-One - The 21St Century Closet	44
Chapter Twenty-Two - Packaphobia	47
Chapter Twenty-Three - I Hate Shapewear!	51
Chapter Twenty-Four - Try It, You'll Like It	53
Chapter Twenty-Five - Yes, It's Hot In Here	55
Chapter Twenty-Six - Beware The Compare	57
Chapter Twenty-Seven - Is There A Skeleton In The Closet?	59
Chapter Twenty-Eight - Lesson Learned	61
Chapter Twenty-Nine - Youniquely Normal	65
Chapter Thirty - Be The Big Picture	67

Chapter One

STOP STRESSING ABOUT DRESSING

    OMG! You now have less than forty-eight hours to figure out what to wear to a soiree. You are certain it will be absolutely no problem for you to find the perfect outfit because it's lurking in your wardrobe. You know there must be something fabulous for you to put on, because you have more than one closet filled with clothes, drawers packed so tightly that opening and closing them often requires Olympic strength, piles of shoes up to your calves, along with an ever-growing population of dust bunnies.

    No problem, right? WRONG. Why? Because you probably don't have the *right* clothes in the right sizes, or you don't yet know how to stop stressing about dressing.

    But wait a minute. Didn't you recently get some new clothes and you loved the way you looked in them? That's why you bought them, after all. Oh, you don't like how you look in them? So why did you buy them? Bet you have been asking yourself these questions for quite some time. How can it be that you keep buying clothes yet still have nothing to wear?

The reason picking out what to buy and wear is stressful and somewhat discouraging is that you don't know what you should choose. Your goal is to find clothing that will make you look your best, effortlessly and easily.

If you believe that you are the only one who feels this way, I think you'll be happy to know that you are definitely not alone. Retailers are hoping you stay that way so women keep stuffing their closets and drawers with more and more until they end up having less and less to actually wear. Use this book to let you know that you are not alone if you are at a loss as to how to change the way you see yourself. Each chapter will be relatable and give you the direction to take so YOU will finally Stop Stressing about Dressing.

Chapter Two

Push 'Em Up!

Would you like to know how to instantly look taller and thinner without buying new clothes, losing weight, or not breathing while holding in your stomach? I know you are thinking that this is impossible, but it isn't, and I'll show you how to do it in less than one minute.

Here is what you need to do: put on a long-sleeved top and get yourself to a full-length mirror. Now push only one of your sleeves up. Do you see it? See the subtle and surprising difference? Notice how you look taller and thinner after simply making your sleeve shorter?

"How can that be?" you ask. Well, the proof is in your reflection. By pushing your sleeves up—go ahead and push the other sleeve up too—you are emphasizing your waistline or creating the illusion of one. Therefore, you look thinner.

The shorter sleeves give the impression of greater height, so now you look taller. Keep in mind that you need this styling trick only if you want to look taller and thinner.

Now if you think you need to get a new top to achieve this result, you are wrong. This trick even works with sweatshirts from your school days or your children's or grandchildren's alma mater. However, it is my goal that when you finish reading this book, you will happily and easily select clothes that will be as comfortable as a sweatshirt but a lot more stylish.

Warning: all of my clients have developed an instinct to push their sleeves up whenever they get dressed, or as soon as they see me walking toward them. You too may now find yourself approaching people you care about and pushing up their sleeves, but trust me; they will thank you for it.

Chapter Three

If Not Now, When?

L'Oréal had it right when they started reminding women, back in 1973, that they were worth it. So why do so many women give more to their families, friends, and even their pets than they give themselves?

Your daughter or granddaughter wants you to buy her bras and panties at Victoria's Secret, and you are buying yours at Kohl's or Target. Of course, this is assuming you have even bothered buying yourself new lingerie within the past five years!

Or your daughter or granddaughter wants exercise clothes from a high-end manufacturer, while you have been wearing the same leggings and T-shirts for years. Even worse, you might actually work out, while the youngster is just looking to strut her stuff without a single squat or sit-up.

Oh, the injustice.

Recently a client told me she had her wake-up call when she realized her barely teenaged daughter had better workout clothes than she did. I had to tell her the truth. Many years ago, I was the woman who, after having spent a fortune at Victoria's Secret for my "budding" daughter, realized that the scales of self-care were tipping in the wrong direction. Something inside of me snapped, and shortly thereafter, I marched myself into a lingerie boutique to treat myself to higher-quality and better-fitting bras simply because I am worth it!

Here's the problem with doing more for others than for us. We are unwittingly making ourselves unhappy by lowering our self-esteem and self-confidence. It is not selfish to acknowledge you are worth the trouble or expense of self-care. On the contrary, it is smart and helpful, as you are teaching your children and spouse that you value and respect yourself, that you are important and not insignificant. If you find that you often deny yourself a decent haircut, coloring, a manicure, new clothes, or even a vacation so you can give more to others, then you are diminishing yourself. When we become smaller, we have less to give from our hearts, and that is really the only place we have so much to give and share.

Chapter Four

Come Clean with Color

Have you ever been asked if you are OK or if you are tired, but you feel perfectly fine? It's not a great feeling when people see you as looking ill or exhausted, is it?

The reason you appear unwell could very well be because of the color you are wearing closest to your face. This can be in your clothing, jewelry, or scarves, whichever you have near your face.

Wearing a color that is wrong for YOU can cause:

- You to look like you have under-eye circles, or for them to look darker
- Your facial lines to seem deeper
- Your skin tone to look yellow, green, or red
- Your eyes to appear dull
- Your hair to seem dull and lifeless
- People to think you are not feeling well
- Your nose to look bigger

And worst of all—horrors—it can cause you to look older.

When you wear the colors that are right for YOU, your:

*Under-eye circles look less pronounced and often seem to disappear

*Facial lines are diminished

*Skin tone has a healthy and radiant glow

*Eyes are bigger, sparkling, and clear

*Hair looks shinier and healthier

*Face will look rested, instead of tired or stressed

*Nose will appear smaller

*Entire appearance will definitely look younger

So how is that possible and what should you do, you ask? First, colors close to the face change the way our skin and eyes look. For example, if I were to wear olive, my skin would look a bit green, my eyes yellow, and my hair dull, and my health would be under considerable scrutiny by those around me.

Many resources are available, online and in print, to give you the guidelines you need to choose colors that are going to flatter you. However, you can start right now by simply being observant.

Put on a top that you rarely wear and look at your eyes and skin tone. Are your eyes sparkling? Do you look refreshed or dull and exhausted? Start paying attention to your initial reaction to your appearance, and NEVER—and I mean never—wear a color because it is in style or your shopping companion loved it. Only wear what works for you and you alone. Please promise me that.

There is great news if you do decide to wear an unflattering color. After a day or two of looking unwell, you can call in sick and no one will question your being under the weather. Just don't tell anyone I told you how to pull this off.

Chapter Five

Fabric or Facelift?

Sit down and fasten your seatbelts, because you won't believe how these tips save you thousands of dollars and get you hundreds of compliments.

If your face has lots of texture, such as wrinkles, lines, and scars, you should avoid wearing smooth fabrics from the waist up. Satin is a good example.

What is she talking about, you ask? Is she out of her mind? The answer to those—and any other questions you may have about this advice—is that the strong contrast between the smooth, flawless fabric and your skin will accentuate the bumps and lines on your face. It may trigger an uncontrollable reflex to tug and pull at your face while staring at your reflection in a magnifying mirror, and you may even vow to call your friend who just had "work" done on her face rather than her home.

You will look like you had a facelift when wearing fabrics that don't bring attention to or exaggerate the lines on your face and eyes. Fabrics like boucle, tweeds, brocade, boiled wool, chenille, corduroy, crepe, and whatever other blends or materials you find that are anything but smooth, will bring attention away from any imperfections. This is likely to cause those around you to ask for the name of your dermatologist.

Note: Prints versus solids are also helpful in distracting from skin that is less than perfectly smooth.

But what if you are asking, "I don't have lines, bumps and wrinkles on my face; what fabrics should I not wear?" Just reverse my advice and wear smooth, crisp fabrics that do not have any texture. This way you will be highlighting your enviable skin.

When it comes to the texture of skin, it is best to duplicate it with the fabrics you choose for your tops and even the scarves that you wear. Now that you're ready for your close-up, you won't feel the need to use that magnifying mirror.

Chapter Six

Let Your Hair Choose What to Wear

Your head may now be spinning, wondering if you have been wearing the wrong colors and fabrics. In fact, your hair just might even be standing up. What can Scarlett possibly say about my hair?

In the previous chapter, we dealt with the texture of your skin and how it impacts your choice of fabrics to wear near your face. The texture of your hair can also influence what tops and scarves you should wear.

For example, if you have curly hair, try on a top or scarf that has ruffles. Notice how the curls are being duplicated and how attractive this looks. Nobody will guess what you have done to look so great, but they will notice the difference.

There is nothing wrong with wearing a top that doesn't have the same texture as your hair, but you're missing out on creating a subtle but very flattering look. Straight hair is fine with a ruffled scarf, but even better with a straighter style.

No need to pull your hair out trying to pick out clothes and accessories to go with your straight or curly hair. Just by noticing whether your locks are straight or curly, you will find yourself becoming more aware of your appearance and creative with your wardrobe.

Chapter Seven

Are You a V-Neck or Round-Neck?

The shape of your face is either complimented or somewhat insulted by the neckline you choose to wear. I bet you have heard that a V-neckline is universally flattering. Sorry to report that, no, a V-neckline is not flattering for every woman. Yes, it can make your neck look longer and seemingly elongate your body, yet a V-neckline may still not be right for you.

For instance, if you have a long face, wear rounder necklines to balance out your facial proportions. If you have a neck that is very long, a V-neck will make you look and feel like Big Bird. Wear a softer and rounder neckline, and you will look as graceful as a ballerina.

I once had a client who was so upset about her double chin that she strongly considered getting cosmetic surgery to even out her proportions. She saw her jawline as the only trouble spot and focused on it each time she looked at her reflection. Then I showed her, in less than thirty seconds, how to make her chin area appear smaller, simply by changing her neckline.

I gave her a V-neck top instead of a round-neck which was, by the way, practically all she had, and her mouth opened wide in amazement. Her double chin seemed to have disappeared, along with those lines that form around our necks, as we age, that resemble the rings in a tree stump. Lovely visual isn't it?

The V-neck diminished her chin issue, because her neckline was no longer drawing attention to the roundness of her face. This is a simple, quick, and inexpensive solution to stop you from pulling back the skin around your chin when you check yourself out in the mirror, and don't you deny that you do that.

Chapter Eight

Have Your Contents Shifted?

  Have you ever heard a flight attendant ask passengers to be cautious when opening the overheard compartments, as the contents may have shifted during the flight? When I heard this on a trip, to work with a client in another state, I immediately knew that this was the best way to explain this. One day, when I was around forty, I went to bed thinking I was looking good in my clothes and I was content with my body.

  The next morning, I seemed to have awakened with rolls, bumps, and bubbles that I swear were not there the night before. How come the jeans and T-shirt I had successfully worn the day before now made me look old and out of shape? What had happened?

  Ladies, I am sorry to report that no matter how hard you exercise or how well you eat, our contents shift while we fly through our lives. This is not cause to grab an oxygen mask, although you may now be hyperventilating. It just means that a few changes need to be made to accommodate the shift. If rolls are obvious, wear clothes that disguise and cover them up. If the shirt and pants you once wore beautifully now expose ruffles and ridges in your waist and thighs, get them out of your closet and replace them with clothes that lie smoothly over the troublesome spots instead of clinging to them for dear life.

Chapter Nine

Size Doesn't Matter

Ever find yourself in your bedroom or a dressing room determined to get into a pair of pants no matter how long it may take to get them on? If the label is showing a size that you have worn before, surely it will fit again because, darn it, your willpower is way bigger than your thighs, right?

Wrong. In the case of finding clothes that fit and flatter, size doesn't and shouldn't matter. Way too often a woman beats herself up because the size she used to wear—or wants to be—is no longer is an option. Rather than vowing, once again, not to eat much that day or actually use your gym membership, try not to focus on the size label. Instead, concentrate on how your clothes fit the body you have.

I am not trying to discourage women from healthy diets and exercise, but if it has been a while since you swore you would lose that post-baby fat, from twenty-five years ago, or the extra weight you gained in college, and you are close to attending your own child's college graduation, isn't it time to let go of the smaller size label and focus on properly fitting into the size you are now?

Imagine a man going into a store looking for a new pair of pants and discovering that the thirty-four-inch waist he typically wears is a bit snug. He doesn't storm out irritated or squeeze into the too-tight pants so he is barely able to walk. Instead, the angel of men's clothing departments, also known as the tailor, descends upon him and his salesperson with his magic tape measure and turns it into a perfectly fitting pair of pants.

Ladies, you too can have your own fit angel, except you have to seek them out in better stores or in your locality. So if the size-ten pants, top, or dress is snug in some spots, go up one size and have a tailor take in the loosely fitting areas. Then you will have clothes that fit like they were made just for you. And, in a sense, you made it all work. Keep in mind that nobody gets a compliment based on the size printed on his or her clothing. Compliments and comfort occur when your clothes fit well and, when needed, they have been tailored for your curves. Being a size six does not equal happiness or success. Having a wardrobe that gives you confidence may open doors for you that can lead you to possibilities beyond your wildest dreams.

I have size-eighteen clients who are far better dressed than the twenty-somethings they work with, because they stopped waiting to lose weight before investing in properly fitting, flattering clothes.

Alert: Try not to have distaste for the larger size labels. One of my clients once did. She hated seeing what size she wore so much that she cut the size tags out of EVERY single piece of clothing she owned. When I got to her home, she had no idea what size any of her clothes really were. It was also interesting that she disliked almost all of her clothes and had not gone shopping for new ones for years. She had complained so much about never having anything to wear, despite a closet full of tagless pieces, that her husband had hired me to end her daily lament.

After I showed her what clothes would look great on her, and convinced her not to worry about size tags, it was time to go shopping for the right clothes. This was a very easy decision to make. What size she should try on was not the problem any longer. So do yourself a favor and think of size tags as being like those tags on mattresses with the warning label: Do Not Remove Under Penalty of Law.

Chapter Ten

End the Trend

At the start of every season, the fashion experts on TV and in magazines tell us what "must haves" we should add to our closets. Perhaps it is a white shirt, black dress, tan trench coat, and animal print shoes or belt. Oh wait! Isn't that what they seem to recommend to women practically every year, despite the fact that tan is a very unflattering color on many women, including myself? Black is harsh on some others, and white can make some people's skin tone look ghostly. Spellcheck may have changed "ghastly" to "ghostly," but there really isn't much of a difference, right?

These experts typically represent a manufacturer or retailer and are there to encourage shopping. Trend purchases are often behind many of those price tags I see hanging on unworn garments in women's closets. Actually, there are a few women who can pull off almost any look, but that is their personal style, and they typically work in the fashion field. These women would never be labeled fashion victims as they are all about being on-trend, and they are in the business of doing so.

But if you are an entrepreneur, stay-at-home mom, lawyer, speaker, writer, decorator, artist, volunteer, or fundraiser—whatever field you are in—you want your unique talents, personality, creativity, and self-confidence to shine. You don't want to advertise the metallic top the fashion stylist on TV claimed you simply MUST wear.

No, you do not have to buy or wear the latest trend to look current or fashionable. Actually, not following the current fad is a style in itself, and one that I personally employ.

This does not mean dressing like you did twenty years

ago, even though you may be lucky enough to still fit into your closet's archives. Nor does dressing to be in style mean wearing crop tops or thigh-high boots just because they are the "must haves" of the season.

Even worse, a woman can look much older when she wears an outfit based on the hottest trend instead of what works best for her body, age, and lifestyle.

The simple trick is to dress to not look old-fashioned rather than wearing the looks of the season. Take, for example, the color orange, which was "the" color a while back. Some women looked like pumpkins in that color, and their skin looked orange as well. No one wants to look like a fruit or vegetable—not ever.

Remember those low-cut pants that caused men, small children, and—oh yes—us ladies, to gasp when the wearer bent over? At least with a plumber, it was worth the offense as we wanted our leaky faucets fixed. It was not so endearing when a woman bent down so we could see the manufacturer label on her underwear.

Chapter Eleven

Don't Shop 'til You Drop

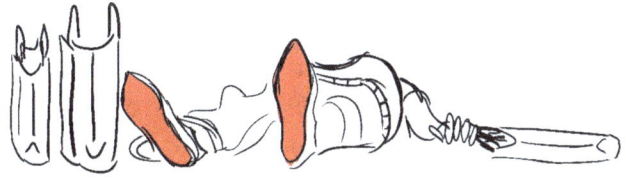

Whether you love or hate to shop for clothes, I suggest a few guidelines to make shopping more productive and much less painful, exhausting, and wasteful.

1. Shop Alone: No friends, sisters, mothers, or mothers-in-law. Why? For starters, I have never met a woman who wants to dress like her mother or mother-in-law. Not ever!

Unless your shopping partner is able to determine what looks great on YOU, and not what she likes, you will end up spending money on items you will be unlikely to wear. I know this because of all the times a client has told me the history of her closet's unworn and unloved mistakes.

As an example, let's say your shopping sidekick loves to wear floral prints in bright neon colors, so she urges you to try on a top or dress that matches her personal tastes. Now she cannot stop shrieking with delight, urging you to buy this colorful beauty, while you look and feel like a tropical drink at a tiki bar.

Despite knowing, in your gut, that this is not what you should buy, you do not want to disappoint your beaming pal and ruin the fun, or—let's just get it over with—ruin the whole day. Besides, the salesperson can't stop telling you how terrific you look. And that leads me to:

2. Beware of Advice from Salespeople: Don't let a complete stranger, who makes commission, tell you how great you look. Yes, your butt might actually look big, but it is doubtful she will tell you the truth.

Of course, there are some great salespeople—and be sure to shop with them whenever possible—but unless you know someone will be completely honest and creative, put on some earplugs and trust your gut. I promise that your first reaction to how you look is the one that counts.

3. Don't Leave Your Dressing Room: There you are in the dressing room, but you need to see how you look from all sides before you can decide if this is the outfit for you. No problem, all you have to do is step out of your dressing room and take a look in the three-way mirror.

Then you hear those reassuring words: "Oh, Honey, that looks wonderful on you!" In case you couldn't hear her, as you were too busy jumping up and down trying to see how you would look in heels, a neighboring customer also tells you how wonderful you look. **SOLD.**

So what if the color is all wrong and you are having a hard time breathing as your lungs and stomach are being compressed by this outfit? Two strangers love it on you and, despite the fact that one of them happens to be on commission, you now love it as well. You love it because their compliments have caused you to unconsciously become attached to it and have clouded your ability to make your own decision.

Be aware that stores deliberately place three-way mirrors in communal spaces so that you get compliments from strangers that will seal the deal.

4. Be Asocial: If you do step out so you can see how you look from behind, follow my advice above and listen to music or pretend to be on a call. Do whatever it takes to avoid being influenced by strangers and, above all, avoid eye contact. OK, I made up that one after having spent my younger years watching too much science fiction on TV.

Here is a segment of an email send to me by a participant in one of my presentations:

PS. I laughed when you suggested that we shop alone, and not with a friend who will dress us in her tastes and not mine. This was my recent experience. A friend we'll call "Floral freak" selected an orange, yep, ORANGE floral top for me and she enthusiastically said it complimented my looks. Upon reflection, I do think it was the top she admired and not me in it. It was half price and we could not resist!

When my wits returned and I was home again with buyer's remorse, I decided to donate it to someone who actually looks good in orange. And that I will. Thanks again!"

Chapter Twelve

Do You Know Where Your Breasts Are?

Remember what Grandma used to look like when she was wearing an old bra or, shudders, no bra at all? Although we get older and gravity is having a big laugh at the expense of our body parts, we can easily lift our breasts to where they belong.

Did you know that when you are wearing poorly fitting old bras you probably look older? Who wants that? Go get a professional bra fitting, and expect to be amazed. Without a properly fitting bra, your waistline appears bigger, clothes don't fit properly, and you look hunched over. None of these seem like desirable options, so head over to a local lingerie shop or major department store. I do prefer a local store, since I like the idea of supporting your community, while they are literally about to support you!

If you have never had a professional bra fitting, you don't know what you're missing. Chances are you are, indeed, wearing the wrong bra size. When you discover what size you really are, you will be delighted at how good you can look in a properly fitting bra.

If it has been a year or more since you replaced your bras, it's time for a professional fitting. I know bras can be very expensive, and it hurts to have to replace them, but odds are that, after one year, they are no longer doing the job they were intended to: keeping you up, centered, and proud! Bras get worn out just like we do after exercise, and keeping breasts up where they should be can be exhausting! Remember that not only will you look better, but you'll also feel a lot better when you see how *uplifting* this experience will be.

So when should you get new bras?

Almost every time I have a wardrobe styling consultation with a client, I ask, "When was the last time you had a bra fitting or bought new bras?"

I remember one new client, in particular, who was about sixty years old and had bras that were clearly past their expiration date. When I showed her, by pulling her straps up, that there was so much space being taken up by her breasts being down, she saw for herself that a few new bras were clearly needed.

I took her to the lingerie department of the store where we had just finished getting her fantastic new clothes, and I left her in the dressing room with the bras the sales associate had given her after measuring her to determine the size and style in which she would look best. Suddenly, I heard a woman screaming, and I quickly realized it was my client. I ran to her dressing room and asked her if she was all right. Turns out, she was shouting with joy. She was so excited because, as she told me, "I didn't know my breasts could look like this again."

So, when should you get a new bra? There are a few key factors to consider:

1. Have you lost or gained ten pounds or more?

2. Do your straps need constant readjustments because the elastic is stretched out?

3. Are your breasts heading further south or going east & west at the same time? Trust me, it happens.

4. Is your posture getting worse?

But here is the best incentive to get a professional bra fitting and a few new bras: you will have a more visible waistline when your breasts are up where they belong. When you lengthen the space between the breasts and hips, you will have a more defined waist and all your clothes will look 100 percent better on you.

Get ready to look younger, taller, and thinner when wearing a great-fitting bra. You will definitely stand taller, look thinner, and feel younger when your bust is up where it was in your teen years but, thankfully, without all the high school drama.

Chapter Thirteen

The Perils of High Heels

Do you try to wear shoes that are a perfect fit, like Cinderella's, or attempt to cram your tootsies into the "perfect" shoe just like her evil stepsisters? Many women are determined to pack their feet into the wrong shoes—which, in itself, is not a natural look—just so they can wear certain styles, despite the truth and consequences.

I remember, years ago, I was shopping at an incredible shoe sale in a very high-end store. There were so many gorgeous shoes and boots all around me, at irresistibly low prices, yet I became frozen as I could not take my eyes off one customer's feet. She was impeccably dressed and had towers of shoeboxes all around her. Her credit card was about to turn to smoke from her huge purchase. But I could not stop staring at those feet. You see, she had just finished testing out another pair of gorgeous, delicate, pointy-toed high heels, and she had looked elegant until she sat down and removed the shoes. Never before had I seen feet like hers. They had bumps all over them, her toes were curled in many directions, and the arches of her feet resembled the Arc de Triumph in Paris.

Please know that I am in no way exaggerating how deformed and unsightly her feet looked. I vowed, right then and there—with the power and conviction of Scarlett O'Hara in *Gone with The Wind*—that as long as I wore shoes, my feet would never be in pain again!

Why would I? I had now seen first-hand, actually first-foot, what happens to women's feet when they are forced into shoes that look pretty but do not return the compliment to the wearer's feet.

Some women are so determined to fit into certain shoes that they are having procedures done, beyond bunion removal, so they can wear designer shoes and high heels. They take extreme measures to wear extreme shoes. Some women even request to have their pinkie toes removed so they can wear designer shoes so high they may get a nosebleed.

Keep in mind that the higher you are, the harder you fall, so how about this wild and crazy thought: what if designers created beautiful shoes to fit our feet, instead of forcing us to fit into shoes that cause deformities, pain, and short tempers!

Thankfully, more and more shoe companies are designing shoes to give comfort, support, and style instead of pain, blisters, and twisted ankles. I have shoes that are comfortable and stylish. Seek out designers and manufacturers that create stylish shoes with padding, extra width, and the ability to hold inserts. No matter what a woman's foot issues are, these days, there are enough shoe styles out there that the orthopedic look is no longer your only option.

Chapter Fourteen

Step Back from the Rack

You decide to do some clothes shopping, and there it is, a top or pair of pants that is practically calling your name. You seem to already know each other so well; after all, it knows just what to whisper to your subconscious mind, hugs you like an old friend, and makes you feel safe, protected, and secure.

Wait a minute! I bet you already have an item in your closet nearly identical to the one you are being attracted to like a magnet. If so, you are not alone. It is very common to be drawn to what we already have, know, and like, even if it isn't any good for you. Remember that boyfriend or girlfriend who made you feel like hell, yet you kept waiting for the phone to ring? Or that potato chip you knew you shouldn't eat because, like the rest of us, you couldn't eat just one? It is typical human behavior to want more of what we already have, although the familiar is not always in our best interests.

Try to step back from the rack, but especially from the black. Women have a tendency to purchase yet another pair of black pants, despite already owning enough pairs to make blackout curtains for your bedroom. Force yourself to move past the black clothes and the things that look like what you already have, and only buy what is NOT like what is already in your wardrobe. If many of your clothes are similar, all your outfits will be as well. Hey, the expression "variety is the spice of life" resonates for a reason, right?

Chapter Fifteen

Divorce, Despair and What to Wear

It happens. Did it happen to you? A special friend? A relative? Often when you least expect or want it, it happens. It is the D-word: Divorce.

So here you are, single again, and questioning everything about yourself, just like you did when you were in high school, except now you are in the school of life. Why was I not good enough? What did I do wrong? Is it because I'm old? Is it because I no longer look the way I did when we first got married? Who would want me now? How can I compete with younger women to find a loving partner? Who would find me attractive?

Then you might start giving yourself some very destructive and self-sabotaging messages, such as:

- Now I'll be alone for the rest of my life.
- I hate the way I look.
- I look tired.
- I look old.
- I look terrible in all my clothes.

I am sure you have had a few damaging inner talks, but I want to tell you to stop talking and start listening. You are never too old to love the way you look. NEVER! The only person you have to impress is yourself and only yourself. When you like what you see in a full-length mirror, others will as well.

I see that sparkle in a woman's eyes when she sees herself

in clothes that transform her from feeling frumpy to fabulous. ALL women can have that sparkle, regardless of their age, size, budget, or marital status. Don't think you have to dress like you are in your thirties to look desirable, as that will backfire in a big way. When women dress like they are a few decades younger, it often makes them look even older and occasionally a bit silly.

Let's get started on getting you going in the right direction in the brand new chapter in your book, and together we can make it a page turner!

Take the following steps to get a fresh start on transforming how you see and feel about yourself:

- Get all new bras, professionally fitted of course, as well as panties. Only you have to know how pretty your lingerie looks... for now.

- Donate or sell clothes that bring up negative or sad emotions. If the dress you wore on a special anniversary or other event makes you feel down, or causes you to sigh out loud, get it out of your home, just like your ex.

- Don't keep the empty closet space your ex left behind as a shrine. One of my clients emptied her ex-husband's custom-made closet, so I suggested turning it into a shoe and handbag closet, which she did. Now she smiles when she opens its doors instead of mourning what once was.

- Try a new hairstyle, but shampoo first. Think, I'm going to wash that man right out of my hair.

- Get a new makeup and skincare routine. Each product that you apply is a form of rejuvenation. YOU deserve to be pampered.

- Get a manicure regularly, or do your own nails. No more getting your hands dirty is required.

- Pick one of your best features and highlight it with your clothes and accessories. This could be your eyes, hair, skin, legs, or even your sense of humor.

- Dress nicely every single time you go out, whether you are walking the dog, buying groceries, going to the library or mall, or getting a root canal. Dress so you won't be embarrassed if you bump into someone you know. Not only will you feel good that you made the effort, you'll look good too.

Use tips from each chapter to choose what to wear and how to wear it. It is never too late to look your best, start over, and look forward. There is a reason nobody walks backward.

Chapter Sixteen

Battling the Bathing Suit Blues

Congratulations! You are finally taking a relaxing vacation to a sunny tropical spot. All you need to pack are a few pairs of shorts or pants, a couple of tops, and a bathing suit.

Cue the music played when the young woman is swimming in the ocean in *Jaws*. The thought of finding and wearing a bathing suit may cause an equal amount of dread and fear, as well as some blood-curdling screams.

Relax a while and let me give you a few tips to get you back in the water, or at least on a lounge chair. I want you to enjoy your time in the sun.

- Do not try on suits that are the same size as your clothes. Don't ask me why, but swimwear sizes do not correspond with clothing sizes. Women need to try one or two sizes up for a flattering and comfortable fit.

- Choose a suit in a color that compliments you. And FYI: avoid white, especially if you plan on getting wet.

White suits will always become see-through. If that doesn't bother you, you are reading the wrong book.

- Highlight your smaller parts with lighter colors and camouflage your somewhat larger parts with darker colors. I use this trick to minimize what I consume at the all-you-can-eat buffet tables or a few too many Pina Coladas.

- Watch your back. No, really, take look and see if the shape of your back is pushing over the edge of your bathing suit. If it is, go for a style with a higher back so more of you is held in.

- Of course you wish you had a smaller waistline, so look for suits that have shirring at the middle. The fabric gathering is a great way to disguise muffin tops and tummy poufs.

- Tuck, lift, and suck. Tuck, lift, and suck. Repeat this mantra each time you put on your suit. Tuck in your breasts, lift up your rear so it is in the bathing suit versus hanging out around the edges, and suck in your stomach when you walk to or get up from your lounge chair.

- Never underestimate or abuse the power of the cover-up. A simple lightweight tank dress or oversized shirt is far more flattering than shorts and a T-shirt and fits so well with pool or beach surroundings.

An afterthought: If the mere idea of wearing a bathing suit still causes you flashes of terror, I have heard Alaska is a lovely place to visit.

Chapter Seventeen

Don't Waste Your Waist

Every woman can have a waistline, but not every woman knows how to emphasize the one she has, or create one that she doesn't have.

A woman's shape can be straight, round, or curvy, but her waist can be wasted—a no-show—if her clothes and accessories don't highlight her existing or I-know-it-must-be-there-somewhere waistline.

Use the following tips to whittle your middle so you can show off your waist, or create the impression that you have one.

- Wear jackets that have rounded corners at the hem, not squared. This gives a woman the look of an hourglass shape instead of a boxy one. No woman should wear clothes that cause her to have the shape of a storage container.

- Put on a tank top that can go under a cardigan or flowing jacket. Start with a belt where a waist would be on an hourglass-shaped woman, whether you are high- or low-waisted. Now put on a short or long cardigan-style sweater, jacket, or some other type of topper over the belted area. Voila, you have a waistline.

- Look for tops and jackets that have princess seams. These seams are slightly curved, giving the illusion of a smaller and shapelier waist. These seams can be in the front and/or back of the garment.

- Waist insets in the back of a jacket, cardigan, or whatever other topper you find give the folks behind you a delightful view of a defined figure.

- Tops and dresses that use color blocking (fabrics are sewn together to create clothing with a few different solid colors) will trick the eye into seeing less of a person than there really is.

- A garment that has darker panels on the sides can magically appear to take inches off of a woman's body.

- A woman can be any size, yet still have a waist area. Granted it is easier for some than others to show it off, but it is not impossible.

- Don't waste your waist simply because you are not the size you dream of being.

Chapter Eighteen

Where Have All the Sleeves Gone?

Do you hate goodbyes? Oh, I don't mean you lament over not seeing someone till you next meet. Do you hate having to wave goodbye, or even hello, because you are self-conscious about your upper arms?

Close to 90 percent of the women I work with despise showing their arms. When the temperature gets above 70 degrees, they form beads of sweat on their foreheads, not from the weather, but in anticipation of either exposing their arms or wearing sweaters and possibly collapsing from heat exhaustion on warm days.

Honestly, a majority of these women do not have upper arms as horrific as they think. Without a strict diet and regular muscle-toning exercises, the upper arms do become less toned as we age. Oh heck, even with the hard work, upper arms on women past the age of fifty start to become, shall we say, less than perfect.

Some solutions are more practical to implement than others, so I suggest skipping my first three.

- Cut yourself off from the rest of the world and stay inside. This way you will never again have to wave your arms or raise your arm to your forehead to shield your eyes from the sun. On windy days, this is particularly a nightmare.

- Wear skin-toned support pantyhose on your arms for a smooth look. However, I must tell you that using your hands becomes extremely difficult and runs are very unsightly on the arms.

- Become the Queen of England so all you are required to do is the royal wave, performed with your elbow below the wrist.

- Look for loosely knitted cotton-type fabric shrugs, cardigans, or other pieces that can be worn over tops and dresses. The loose weave will make them airy and comfortable in warmer weather. Some department stores have these in their scarf and accessory departments.

- Ask sales associates to show you clothes with short or long sleeves. If they are unavailable, ask to speak to the manager and let him or her know that the selection does not include what you need. Just think about how well how the squeaky wheel theory will work in this instance.

- Scour the internet searching for tops and dresses in the sleeve length you desire. They are out there although stores might not have them in stock. Example: search for "blue dress, short sleeves, V-neck."

- Be sure that the sleeves, straps, or armholes of your clothes are not too tight. This will prevent your upper body and arms from spilling over and giving the impression that there is more of you in places than there actually is.

- Distract yourself and others from your arms by wearing flattering, unusual, or whimsical necklaces. Lightly woven scarves are another way to distract people's eyes and your self-image away from your arms. If the scarf has enough fabric, you could even let it drape on your shoulders to cover up and distract.

Above all, don't let the fact that your arms look more like the "before" picture in an exercise program advertisement than the "after" dissuade you from getting out and being friendly and ready to throw caution, not your arms, to the wind.

Note at how color, necklines and style actually make each woman look younger, thinner and taller. Even better, they no longer are Stressing About Dressing

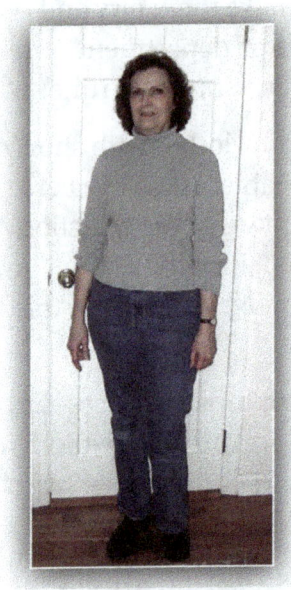

Before   **After**

Stop Stressing About Dressing

Before   **After**

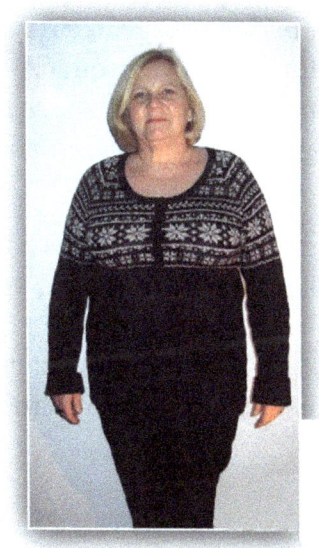

Chapter Nineteen

Back Bumps and Lumps

Not until I tried on a dress that was a tiny bit snug and turned around to see what my daughter was laughing at, did I became highly aware of what was going on behind me. There, in the mirror, was a reflection of what looked like some mighty fine breast implants, but they were on the wrong side of my body! I had back cleavage, and I laughed along with my daughter who, at that point, was practically rolling on the floor.

I regret to this day that I did not photograph my impressive back monstrosities and am convinced that my front cleavage was quite jealous of the competition. There was no turning back. My clients will never have exposed back fat or back cleavage. Not on my watch.

Now it's time to learn what to do. Remember that back fat is common but can be contained or minimized when following these tips:

- Go up one size if you get back cleavage in a dress, bathing suit, or exercise top. When you squeeze yourself into a piece of clothing, parts of you escape to another part of your body and bear a resemblance to a lava lamp.
- If a top or dress is a little too big, but your back fat is hidden and contained, shorten the straps and take in any spot that needs to be adjusted for a perfect fit. My clients are always amazed at how simply shortening tops at the shoulder seams transforms the fit and look of their clothing.

- If you are broad-shouldered, have back fat, or both, only wear wide straps, as they are in proportion to your shape. Avoid racer back styles at all costs, as they create disturbing-looking back cleavage and back fat spillage.

- Get a professional bra fitting. A bra in the wrong size or with the wrong fit can create oodles of puddles and accentuate or create back cleavage and back fat—it can be almost as bad as no bra at all.

- Always look at what is happening behind you and have a sense of humor about all the directions our bodies can go when wearing the wrong clothes and lingerie. It is NEVER the fault of your shape, but rather the wrong clothes for your body.

Chapter 20
Frumpy or Fabulous?
Six Ways for Women Over 50
To Improve Their Professional and Personal Image

Does your image say:

- Hire me or fire me?
- Promote me or demote me?
- Date me or hate me?

These are good questions for women, especially those over fifty, to ask themselves, as their bodies and self-esteem are rapidly changing. Often they do not realize their image is not as good as it could be and should be to gain both professional and personal advantages.

What once fit or looked good on them no longer seems to be as flattering. Makeup, hairstyles, and hair colors that seem to add years to their look, instead of making them appear younger, are not right for women over fifty.

These issues can keep a woman from being hired, promoted, or even asked out if she is re-entering the dreaded dating world.

The great news is that a woman over fifty can actually look better than she did in her younger years—and have more professional and personal success than she has ever imagined—simply by making a few important changes in her appearance.

Try implementing these six strategies to improve your image and discover how you can actually look better than you have in years.

- Stop wearing clothing that is too tight or too big for you. Wearing improperly fitting clothes is uncomfortable, makes you appear older, and sends the message that you do not pay attention to yourself and your career. If your seams are straining or your pants are too loose, please make finding the right clothes a top priority!

- Wear less makeup then you did back in your 20's, or wear some makeup if you never have before. Seek a balance so you don't look like you are wearing a mask and don't appear that you don't even bother with the effort of applying some makeup. Sometimes mascara and lipstick are all that you need.

- Don't wear outdated clothes, as that guarantees that you will look older, out of date, stuck in the past, and incapable of changing with the times. Just because it still fits does not mean it should still be worn.

- Stay on top of your roots. Not your family roots, but your hair regrowth. Do not let it be obvious that you are covering up gray hair. Between salon visits, many touchup products are available to cover up the gray or match your highlights.

- Find out what clothes work best for your particular body shape and which manufacturers design clothing for your particular shape.

- Don't wear shoes that look like they are for problem feet. There are so many choices now in footwear that looks stylish but offers comfort and discreet support for a variety of orthopedic needs.

Making these changes will be a big factor in professional and personal success and fulfillment for a woman over fifty. Make a few simple changes and get those people under fifty to look over their shoulders at you. After all you are wiser, more confident, and more experienced, and now you are a much better dresser too.

Chapter Twenty-One

The 21st Century Closet

For Sale: Wedding Dress Worn Once by Mistake

I read this ad in a local paper, over twenty-five years ago, and I have never forgotten it. How could I? Besides admiring this former bride's excellent advertising skills, I saw that there was a lesson to be learned from her less-than-happily-ever-after ending.

THE LESSON:

1. Divorce the clothing and accessories that you no longer can or should wear. You can start by getting to know your clothes and shoes in a more meaningful way.

2. Pick about ten items from your closet that you have ignored and ask yourself the following questions:

- How do I feel when I wear it?
- Does it accentuate or diminish a part of my body I wish were bigger or smaller?
- Is it in poor condition? Stains, holes, or missing buttons?
- Do I feel frumpy or fabulous when I wear it?

    Can I eat anything I want while wearing it?

Now's the time to take just thirty minutes to analyze those questionable pieces, then take a deep breath and walk down the aisle to a relationship you have always dreamed of having with your closet and the clothes in it. Follow the steps below and transform your relationship with your wardrobe into a love affair that never ends, with a partner who never talks back.

STEP ONE: Donate all of your tops that are too short.

Years ago, manufacturers made all tops on the short side. Remember the showing-the-tummy fashion phase? These short tops are not usually flattering or comfortable. They are, however, taking up precious space in your closet. Only keep the pullovers or button-down tops that reach below your waist. Chances are those are the only ones you will really wear. So go ahead and get those shorties out of there!

STEP TWO: Review all your pants and skirts to see if any are too short for you now.

The best skirt length for most women is right at the top or middle of the knee. Anything too long or short will probably look dated and not be flattering. The skirts that fall into that category probably have not even been worn in years anyway, right? Full-length skirts and dresses are fine as long as they are not from another decade and the look is flattering and not aging.

The best pants length is long enough not to show your ankles when standing. Otherwise your legs will look awkwardly short. It will also visually widen your body and—well here is that word again—look dated.

So how simple is this maneuver? Very simple indeed.

Take out the tops, skirts, and pants that are too short, and you will already see a huge difference in your ability to find what you are looking for and create more outfits.

STEP THREE: Almost all of my clients have clothes from the 80's and the 90's in their closets, and each one wonders if she is the only woman who has held onto these antiques. To be perfectly sure that you are free of the last century, remove any top that has shoulder pads or looks like it was worn on a TV show from that time period.

As entertaining as the 80's and 90's were in terms of fashion, there truly are very few pieces that one should save to wear to a theme party.

Your clothes and accessories should have been bought in a year starting with a two. I am not talking about wearable vintage pieces, but the things that are simply taking up space in your closet and drawers. Crowding your closet with old clothing makes it difficult to find clothes that are wearable and flattering.

STEP FOUR: If any of your clothing is stained, has holes, or is in non-flattering colors or fits, pull it out of your closet and drawers. You should only wear clothes and accessories that make you look and feel good. Nothing that cannot be worn or is only there to remind you of times gone by should take up space. Also, use the same hangers for all your clothes, and your closet will look bigger and more organized.

AND FINALLY: If you take the time to follow these simple steps, you will save many hours of trying to get through the jungle of your closet to find what will work for you. You will go from closet chaos to wardrobe bliss in a short period of time. After all, happiness is having a closet filled with clothes you'll actually wear.

Chapter Twenty-Two

Packaphobia

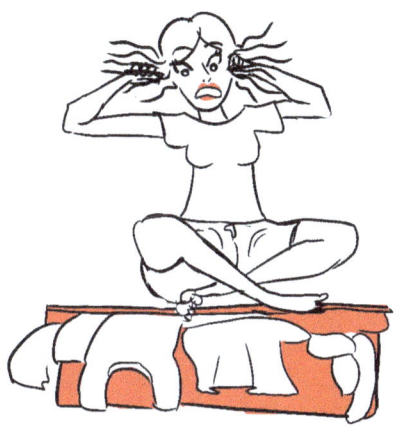

Packaphobia: The fear or dislike of deciding which clothes to pack, or the inability to pack the number of items one really needs.

Please do not be alarmed that you and many other women you may know suffer from this stress-provoking condition. It is nothing to be ashamed of and can easily be treated. Luckily for you, I have a cure.

I have packed for a week while traveling through Europe and throughout the United States, with temperatures ranging from the high 90's to the low 60's. The trick to not over-packing, or getting overly anxious about not packing enough, is to select clothes and accessories that can be mixed and matched. Simply adding a scarf or changing your jewelry can transform many outfits.

Here is what I pack, and I make all the pieces interchangeable to create more outfits that I could possibly wear in a seven- to ten-day period. Oh, and did I mention that I only use a carry-on suitcase? I love experiencing the joy of walking off a plane, bypassing luggage claim, and getting my vacation or business trip off to an immediate start.

For cooler and rainy destinations, I take the following:

- One pair of white denim straight-legged jeans
- One pair of dark denim straight-legged jeans
- One tunic top that can be worn with either pair of pants
- One tan casual pencil skirt
- Two sleeveless tops that can be worn with all bottoms
- Three long-sleeved tops that can be worn with all bottoms
- One sleeveless long dress
- One jacket that can be worn over my dress and all tops except for the tunic
- One scarf
- Two pairs of sandals (one for rainy days one to be used as slippers in the hotel)
- One pair of sneaker-like shoes for lots of sightseeing
- Travel-sized toiletries
- Three necklaces
- Three pairs of earrings
- One watch
- One pair of pajamas
- Two bras
- Four pairs of panties

- One pair of socks
- One handbag
- Travel size toiletries
- One small umbrella

I wear the dark jeans, one sleeveless top, the jacket, sandals, and scarf on plane rides.

For warmer temperatures, I take the following:

- Two dresses
- White jeans
- Blue denim Bermuda shorts
- White shorts
- Orange/white top
- Blue/white top
- Two blue tops
- Two multi-colored tops
- T-shirt for hanging out
- One blue and white infinity scarf that can be worn as a shawl or draped over my shoulders
- One pair of sneakers for the gym
- Blue and white sandals
- Orange sandals
- Flip-flops for the pool and to be my slippers
- One bathing suit
- Two exercise tops

- One pair of socks
- One pair of Capri-length leggings for exercise
- One pair of pajamas
- Travel-sized toiletries
- Three pairs of earrings
- One necklace
- One watch
- One nightgown
- Two bras
- Four pairs of panties
- One handbag

    I wear the long dress and blue and white sandals, along with the scarf, for plane rides. I also highly recommend picking clothes made with synthetic blend fabrics, which resist wrinkling and dry quickly. They also take up less room than cotton and wool does, and are easier to wear when layering. I wash my synthetic blend clothes in the sink with shampoo, so I can have clean clothes and underwear, as needed, while traveling.

    I like to carry an oversized bag that holds my regular handbag, jewelry, and computer or tablet, and I always have room to spare so I can bring home a few unique finds. Of course you can travel with a larger suitcase and hope it shows up at baggage claim, but why bother if you can avoid doing so? But if you simply cannot bring yourself to travel so lightly, the advice I gave you also applies to checked luggage, as long as your suitcases arrive at your destination the same time that you do.

    One woman followed my tips for her wedding and honeymoon, except she carried her wedding dress on board. Trust me, if a bride can do it, so can you.

Chapter Twenty-Three

I Hate Shapewear!

I am embarrassed to admit it, but I was weak and succumbed to peer pressure many years ago. Everybody else seemed to be doing it, so it must be the right thing to do, so I did. Yes, I bought shapewear. Please don't judge me harshly for having tried to wear the very thing I now advise other women to avoid.

It all starts innocently enough, and typically with the following thought: "This dress will be perfect if I wear Spanx shape wear." If I had a dollar for each time I have heard a woman say this, I would have enough money to buy a beach house on an exotic island.

Have you ever thought that putting on a compression garment would solve the problem of your body parts not being as flat and stable as you would like? Somehow many of our body parts have slowly evolved into bowls of jelly, with all the jiggles and wiggles that can make us dizzy and distressed.

I don't know about you, but I hate shapewear. As far as I am concerned, it might as well be called torture-wear. It all started when I bought high-waisted shapewear panties that went from my belly button down to the middle of my thighs, because all the other girls were doing it. I thought my body would rival that of an underwear model, once I had eased my bandaged body into the dress I was hoping to pull off without a hint of excess fat.

And then there I was with a stomach as flat as a board, upper thighs smooth as sheets of ice, and my extra blubber billowing out over the waistband and below the bottom bands on my thighs. I looked like a living lava lamp, oozing and swirling up and down along the middle of my body. Somehow I had a gained a "wedgie" in my muffin top. How is that even possible?

And don't get me started about the struggle to get in and out of that thing. Clearly this was not the solution to my need to fit into that beautiful dress. I had to make a decision and stick with it, instead of my excess flesh staying stuck to the spandex of that darn two-foot-long panty.

My solution was to buy a dress that fit me, as an alternative to my trying to fit into it. By simply choosing a style that works with one's body shape, instead of fighting it, you and I can look and feel better, breathe easier, and literally have room for dessert!

Chapter Twenty-Four

Try It, You'll Like It

There you are, aimlessly wandering through the clothing department with that deer-in-the-headlights look. It appears that you are trying to find something, anything, new and flattering to wear.

You wander from rack to rack, quickly getting discouraged as you are now convinced that there is nothing in the store, or the entire world of apparel, that is right for you. Are these some of the thoughts running through your mind?

- Everything is for thinner bodies.

- Everything is for younger bodies.

- Everything looks the same.

- Everything looks ugly.

- Everything is too expensive.

- Everything looks too cheap.

- Nothing ever fits perfectly.

- Everything makes me look fat.

- Why can other women find clothes that they look good in and I can't?

These negative thoughts are common and destructive. The thoughts that often strike us, when surrounded by clothes, can cause mad dashes to the supermarket, straight to the cookie or ice cream aisle. Clothes shopping can be overwhelming, as there is so much to choose from. Just being under unflattering dressing room lights, dealing with over-eager or non-existent salespeople, and "perfect"-sized mannequins can bring about a wave of unexpected sadness. But worst of all, not knowing where to go, in the store, to find clothes that will, indeed, look good often causes an inner shutdown, thereby denying you the very thing you came for... new clothes.

There are many clothes that will suit you, and I know this for a fact because I find them for my clients every time I shop for them. Since I know clothing, styles, and fit like the back of my hand, I do not get overwhelmed. Actually, I love the thrill of the hunt to find outfits that will make my client smile at her reflection, wearing clothing she never would have picked out for herself. My clients always buy the pieces I place in their dressing rooms because I know what works for them. I have only one rule when shopping with my clients: you must try on what I choose. In other words, try it, you'll like it. And they do.

Follow the tips I give you in this book, and you will go from being overwhelmed and super-stressed, in a large clothing department, to being focused and confident.

Chapter Twenty-Five

YES, It's Hot in Here

It can be below thirty degrees outside, and you have turned on the air conditioning full blast. You are having hot flashes, and you can feel the steam coming up around your face and neck, even as you stick your head inside your freezer.

No matter how many times you ask, "Is it hot in here?" you will probably be the only one who feels the heat growing within. You are hormonally challenged, and those flashes are not lukewarm—they are HOT, HOT, HOT.

So how does one handle hot flashes when in the company of others? Must you spend your free time alone, walking back and forth in the freezer aisle of your local supermarket? After all, you can't strip down in public to make a statement about your overheated condition.

When it comes to knowing what to wear, I go for layers, and lots of them.

- Consider wearing sleeveless tops under long-sleeved tops or jackets. You can wear all of your summer tops under jackets in the winter, so when you peel away, you won't risk getting arrested for indecent exposure.

- Add a scarf. This accessory instantly "winterizes" your outfit and can quickly be whisked away as soon as prickly hot tingling starts to pierce your skin.

- Avoid wearing sweaters as your first layer. You won't have the option of peeling off a layer of clothes, and you will end up having to sit and soak in sweat in public.

- Don't wear turtlenecks or other tops that "choke" the neck. Think how guilty you will feel tugging at your collar like a married man trying to explain where he was all night.

Like waves in an ocean, hot flashes come and go, often knocking down your spirit and gusto. So to avoid getting 'wet,' plan ahead so that you can peel off a layer or two and keep your cool.

Chapter Twenty-Six

Beware the Compare

As I sat in the dermatologist's exam room, waiting for a routine checkup, I could not help but notice the "before" and "after" photos strategically placed in front of me. This collection of facial transformations made it really hard to avert my eyes. It was much like an accident on a highway, where everyone feels the need to slow down and stare. I was thankful that they were not the victims of an unfortunate vehicle incident. Yet I could not help but notice how much better these women looked in the "after" photos. I realized that the fact that those pictures were placed directly at eye level was no accident.

In each case, the first woman had deep lines, known as nasolabial folds—commonly known as laugh lines—from her nose down to her mouth. The second seemed to have the number 111 stamped on her forehead, but they were actually deep furrows. And finally, the third had a loose and saggy chin. However, the after photos, showcasing the results of using fillers—or whatever other potions are conveniently available in this doctor's office—made these women look great!

As intended, they all looked new and improved, and then I made a huge mistake. I slowly turned to look at my own reflection in a mirror that just so happened to be on the wall right next to me. What were the odds of that happening? Now the "accident" that I could not keep my eyes away from was my face, and I looked terrible. I was a "before" shot, before I even knew it.

I was jolted out of my misery when the door opened and the doctor stepped in. After my exam—and no, I did not ask about the filler products—I headed off to the bathroom. As I washed my hands, I glanced up and saw my reflection. I didn't look nearly as bad as I had in the doctor's exam room. Was it the magnificent lighting in the ladies' room that made the difference? I highly doubt it. But I realized that the power of suggestion, deliberately created in his office, was extremely powerful.

Next time I have an appointment with a doctor, I just may turn those mind games off and avoid staring at the before and after photos. Women already have a hard enough time being compared to "perfect" women on the big screen or TV, so it is up to us to turn off that state of mind.

Chapter Twenty-Seven

Is There a Skeleton in the Closet?

A friend of mine, let's call her Phyllis, decided she wanted to "crash" her grown son's Halloween party. Oh, but who to be and what to wear? Phyllis uses a cane, on occasion, for an old back injury, and she chose it as her inspiration to attend her son's soiree as an elderly grandmother visiting from Boca Raton, Florida.

Naturally, she thought she would need to go shopping at a thrift shop or Goodwill to find clothing and accessories to convey the stereotype of an older woman who hasn't updated her style—and her wardrobe—in a very long time. Instead she dug through clothing racks and found a gold lamé blouse, circa 1975 Saturday Night Live, with a giant pointy collar and a shimmer reminiscent of a 1950's Christmas tree bedecked with tinsel.

Perfect!

Next, she scoured the boxes of costume jewelry and came up with oversized gaudy sparkly earrings that were so wrong, yet so right for her costume creation.

The night of the party, she donned her fabulous finds, drew on exaggerated eyebrows, applied lipstick as though her eyes were closed, hunched over, and stood in front of her mirror, completely satisfied with her over-the-top ensemble. She was delightfully unrecognizable and perfectly dressed to invite stares and laughter.

Just one little twist to this story: Phyllis never needed to go out of her home to find her costume as, unfortunately, she had all she needed right at home! Those racks she scoured were in her spare bedroom, and the boxes of unworn jewelry were in her bedroom drawers.

The lesson to learn is that if you can create a costume from your own old unworn clothes and accessories, there is clearly something spooky going on in your home. It is time to remove the clothes that really should be donated to a charity and clean out the cobwebs made out of your threads.

Note: This is a true story and not a scary campfire tale.

Chapter Twenty-Eight

Lesson Learned

Have you ever heard that you should never leave the house without making an effort to look good, because you never know who you may bump into? How about, because you never know when you may have the wrong date for a speaking engagement? Oh, please read on, as this story gets very interesting.

I was asked to speak to a group of men and women in Danbury, Connecticut. They were in a profession that requires their photos to be used on business cards and correspondence. My talk was to offer advice on how to choose the right clothes, so that their professionalism and skills shine through in their headshots.

Perhaps the first hint that this presentation was not going to run smoothly was the description of my presentation:

Your Profile Photo Is Talking

And other secrets of effective online marketing

Presenter: Scarlett Johannsen, Image Consultant and Online Marketing Expert

Scarlett Johannsen? Are you kidding me? These attendees are being told that a highly talented and beautiful Hollywood actress would be giving them personal and business image advice!

Can you imagine how quickly I contacted the person in charge of this event to ask her to identify the speaker as myself, Scarlett De Bease? Seconds—that's how long it took me to reach out and request a correction.

Fortunately for me, I was going to get credit for my own presentation. Unfortunately for the attendees, they were not going to meet Scarlett Johannsen.

Once I'd corrected the "I am not *that* Scarlett" issue, I went back to working on my presentation, selecting the best "before" and "after" photos to represent my tips and carefully writing out my personalized talking points. I even made an appointment to get my hair styled, cut, and colored the day before the scheduled presentation, so what else could possibly go wrong?

With twenty-four hours to go 'til "showtime," I left the hair salon and started driving to meet a friend for lunch in Mahopac, New York. As I was getting close to our meeting point, and my stomach was grumbling, I noticed that the organizer for my talk the next day had left me a voicemail stating that if I needed directions to the event location, I could just give her a ring. Of course I didn't need directions, as I have a GPS.

Again, what can go wrong?

Just as I pulled into a parking spot to meet my friend, the organizer called again, and this time I answered. She wanted to know if I was lost. It was now noon.

I was beginning to shake, stutter, and sweat. She wanted to know when I would get there, as my time to present was only thirty minutes away.

I asked, with my mind racing, "You mean today?"

"Yes, didn't you see the date in the announcement?" She was referring to the invitation stating that Scarlett Johannsen would be speaking. All I could do was say "I will drive over now" and "I'm sorry, I'm so sorry" over and over again.

I ran into the restaurant to tell my friend that I could not stay, and I ran out, jumped into my car, and started to drive home to pick up my computer with the slide presentation that

I had worked on for a week. Oh, did I say drive? More like race. Not only would I have to grab my computer, I would also need to change my pants, as I was wearing jeans, and put on more makeup.

While driving much faster than I should, I berated myself for having made such a huge mistake. I realized that if I were to go to my New York home before heading to Connecticut, I would arrive after the attendees had already left. So I turned my car toward Connecticut and decided to wing it. I would ask them to go to my website to see the "before" and "after" photos of a few of my clients, and I would improvise my talk. I made a forty-five-minute ride into a thirty-minute one, and I am not proud of it.

Did I mention that I was wearing jeans? Remember, I had just had my hair colored. Well, you know that bit of color that remains along the hairline after color is applied? So I arrived, dressed nicely but in jeans, which is not proper attire when presenting to professionals, little makeup, a band of brown on my face, no visual presentation, and not a not a single piece of paper with notes to guide myself.

After apologizing profusely to the group for my Hollywood-style tardiness and for not being Scarlett Johannsen, I asked them all to use their smartphones or tablets to see my photos, and I proceeded to present and answer questions from my audience.

When my presentation ended—and, if I may say so, it went very well—I was slightly calmer but still extremely upset with myself. I am a professional, and looking and acting anything other than one is simply unacceptable to me.

As I made my way around the room saying goodbye, one of the other organizers responded to yet another one of my apologies with this: "Well, in your defense, the original date was tomorrow."

I stood there nodding, and confused. My heart was still not beating properly, and I was simply out of sorts. Frankly, I was a mess inside while doing my best to be polished on the outside. I kept asking myself, "How could I have not changed the date on my calendar?"

I drove straight home, as all I wanted to do was throw on a bathrobe and hide under the covers of my bed. Instead, as soon as I got home I opened my computer and searched, over and over, to find the email informing me of the date change. Can you guess what I found? There was no such email. I was NEVER informed of the date change. As a matter of fact, the only time the new date was sent to me was on the invitation stating Scarlett Johannsen would be speaking.

Note to self:

- Confirm details with a phone call in addition to an email.
- Know your material well enough so you can present anytime and anywhere.
- Don't leave your home without being dressed in such a way that if you were to bump into that loser who once broke your heart, they would quickly regret their stupid mistake.

Chapter Twenty-Nine

YOUniquely Normal

Each time I speak with a new client before scheduling our first consultation, whether on the phone or in person, I ask her to tell me what her dressing dreams and dilemmas may be. What strikes me every time is that her answers are "their" answers, and most likely yours as well:

- She just wants to easily know what to wear and stop leaving piles of rejected outfits on her bed.

- She wants to feel confident and relaxed about her appearance.

- She wants to be able to cover up her tummy, as it is not as flat as it used to be. Okay, it never was truly flat, but it sure was a heck of a lot flatter than it is now.

- She has come to terms with the fact that she will never be as thin as she was ten years ago, and the time has come to throw in the towel and ditch the all-black look.

- She wants to be able to go into a store and come home with clothes that she'll actually wear and not regret buying.

- She wants to not feel frumpy, old, and unattractive.

- She has a closet full of clothes and wants my help in creating calm out of chaos. She just wants to know for sure what she should and shouldn't be wearing, so she can lovingly let go of memories, good and bad, made out of fabric.

- She is exhausted from feeling like she looks old but doesn't feel old.

Each and every woman has the same concerns, yet they are unique to her. She is Uniquely Normal.

Chapter Thirty

Be the Big Picture

Magnifying mirrors are as much a woman's friend as her enemy. While you are exploring your face with the same focus Christopher Columbus may have had when looking for new worlds, you are discovering blackheads, misplaced and unwanted hairs, lines, spots, shadows, etc. Often these "hidden treasures" are practically screaming at us as we examine our faces in those magnifying wonders of amplified reflection.

However, nobody sees what you see in your close-up, especially if other women who are over forty surround you. Unless they all have their reading glasses on, and are examining your face like CSI investigators, they don't see what you see. Take comfort in knowing that there are ways to hide the evidence, and stop feeling like a walking and talking crime scene.

Instead of focusing excessively on the little things, look at the "big picture," which is basically your total image as reflected in a full-length mirror.

If needed, use a magnification mirror only for plucking and eyeliner and mascara application but not for critiquing, picking, and popping, however tempting. Believe me, I know that is easier said than done, and I have the scars to prove it.

Use a full-length mirror to see how you really look, instead of that torturous mini-funhouse magnifier. From your earrings down to your shoes, your entire outfit will supersede a wrinkle or sag.

Wearing flattering clothes will diminish your perceived and actual flaws. There are many ways to look great without magnification and manipulation through plastic surgery. I know this as my clients and I use them every day. Knowing what works best on you will distract your eyes from the small things, and help you see and love the big picture.

THE END

www.ingramcontent.com/pod-product-compliance
Lightning Source LLC
Chambersburg PA
CBHW071541080526
44588CB00011B/1747